Laugh & Learn Too!
Cartoon Features

Laugh & Learn Too! Cartoon Features

For Church Publications

Eddie Eddings

Baker Books
A Division of Baker Book House Co
Grand Rapids, Michigan 49516

© 1993 by Eddie Eddings

Published by Baker Books
a division of Baker Book House Company
P.O. Box 6287, Grand Rapids, MI 49516–6287

ISBN 0-8010-3221-0

Printed in the United States of America

All rights reserved. Selections may be used by churches and other nonprofit organizations without permission from the publisher. If such use involves 1,000 copies or more, each copy must cite the source (title, author/compiler, publisher, date of publication). All other uses (e.g., reproduction as a whole for giveaway or resale, and reproduction of selections in or on any commercial publication or product) require written permission from the publisher.

To
my mother
Eva Tobola
Who believed in me
even at my lowest
and to
the professors and students
of Criswell College

Contents

Acknowledgments	9
Introduction	11
Cartoons	13
Did You Know? Features	33
Bible Quizzes	63
The Illustrated Spurgeon	85

Acknowledgments

Special thanks to
Mike and Bob Ross
of Pilgrim Publications
for the box of
Spurgeon material

to
Curt Daniel
of Believers Chapel
in Dallas

to
Andy Raiford
pastor of
Great Commission Church
Lubbock, Texas
for his brotherly love
and encouragement

and to
my wife
Mary
for her love
and understanding

Introduction

Someone well said, "My conversion is due to myself and God. I fought against God with all my might, and he did the rest." This describes my sudden conversion as well. My "B.C." years were pocked with sin and grief. I did all I could to fulfill my carnal ambitions. Thinking I would always be a musician, I chucked high school to devote myself to rock and roll, rhythm and blues, and drugs. At the age of fifteen I was making good money and squandering it on myself. "Getting high" was my top priority. I was jailed eventually, hospitalized, and committed to a mental institution because of my suicidal inclinations.

When released, I continued pursuing the same activities. I did all I could do to escape reality. I was running ... running from myself ... running from my past ... and without realizing it at the time running straight into the hands of God!

I now know the Lord was setting up all the roadblocks, detours, and dead-ends in my life, leading me through a hopeless maze into a direct confrontation with his Son, Jesus Christ! Hebrews 1:14 declares that God sends his angels to render service to "those who will inherit salvation." He was surely doing that in my tangled life! One night, while alone in my room, I could run no longer. I reached out to the Lord and cried in desperation for him to save me from a life misspent. He heard my plea and miraculously and instantly transformed me. *I will never be the same.*

Eddie Eddings

Cartoons

EASY-TO-COME-BY BOOK REVIEWS

COUNT ZINZENDORF AND HIS ALL MORAVIAN JAZZ BAND

JOHN WESLEY WORKS ON A MIME TECHNIQUE IN THE PRIVACY OF A WOODED GLEN

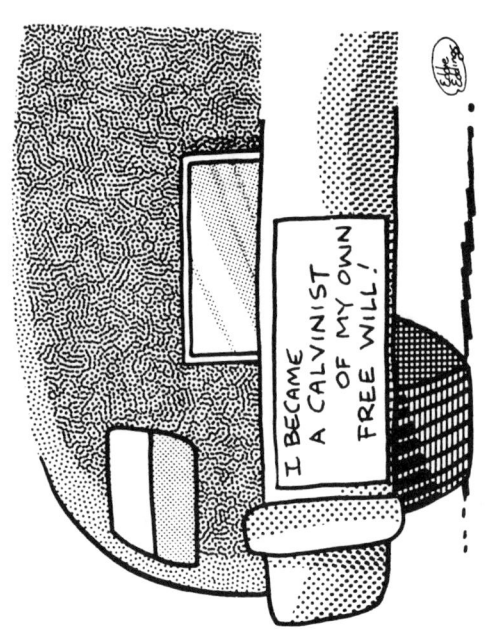
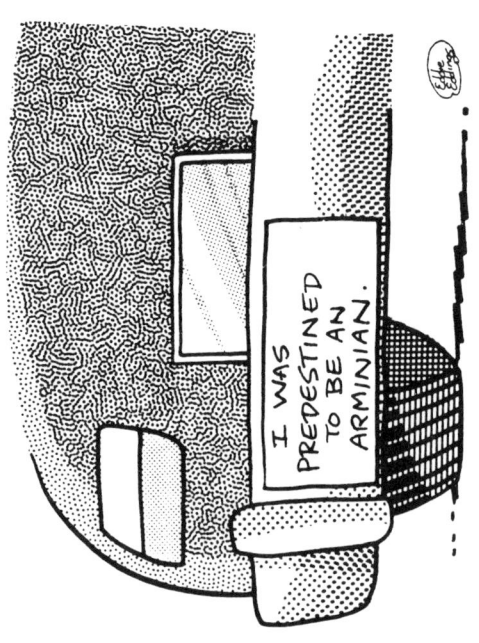

SPURGEON SELLING HIS FAVORITE DESSERT

BOBO SCHLEIERMACHER and DOOFUS KIERKEGAARD by Eddie Eddings

Did You Know? Features

Did You Know?
by Eddie Eddings

GEORGE MATHESON (1842-1906) Gradually went blind as a teenager. His fiancé broke the engagement because she did not want to marry a blind man; he stayed a lifelong bachelor. He went on to earn several college degrees, pastor churches, dictate many devotional works and theology books. Years later, when his sister married, he was reminded of his old fiancé and wrote the hymn, "O Love That Will Not Let Me Go," about the love of Jesus.

Did You Know?
by Eddie Eddings

"We must not live only to live."
— Richard Sibbes

"The sermons most needed today are sermons in shoes."
— C.H. Spurgeon

"I had rather be fully understood by ten than admired by ten thousand."
— Jonathan Edwards

"God's wounds cure; sin's kisses kill."
— William Gurnall

When you pray, there is a clash of arms in the heavenly sphere.

DID YOU KNOW?

SABINE BARING-GOULD (1834-1924) WROTE "ONWARD, CHRISTIAN SOLDIERS" ORIGINALLY AS A MARCHING SONG FOR A CHRISTIAN CHILDREN'S PARADE! HE WAS A PIONEER IN THE COLLECTION OF ENGLISH FOLK SONGS, A COMPOSER OF 2 BOOKS OF HYMNS, AND WROTE A 15-VOLUME SET ENTITLED "LIVES OF THE SAINTS." — THE CATALOG OF THE BRITISH MUSEUM LISTS MORE TITLES BY HIM THAN ANY OTHER WRITER OF HIS ERA! HE WROTE A TOTAL OF 93 BOOKS.

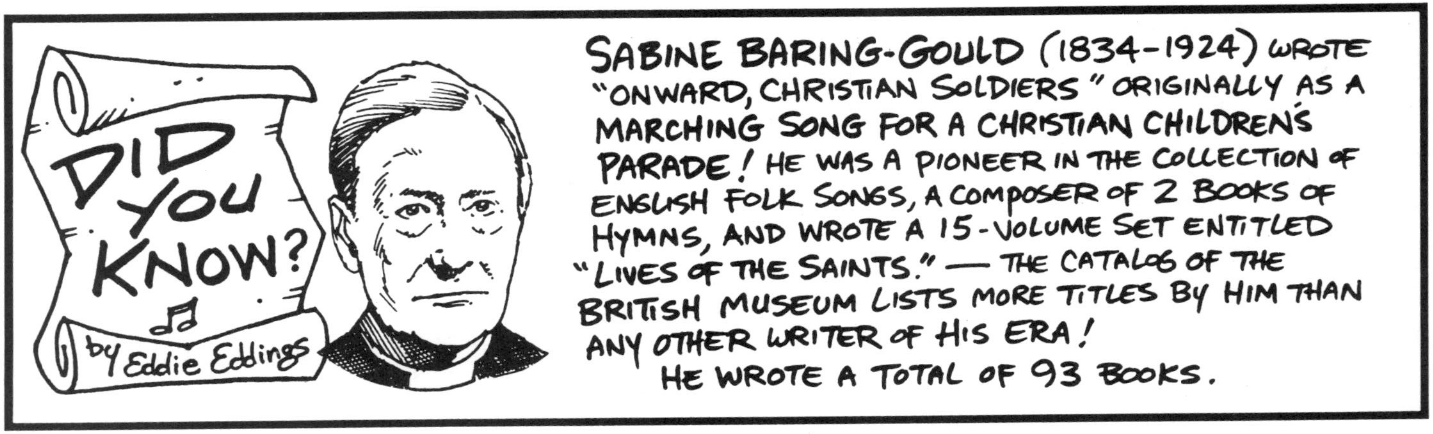

by Eddie Eddings

THE HARDENING OF PHARAOH'S HEART:

THE BOOK OF EXODUS REFERS TO THE HARDENING OF PHARAOH'S HEART **18** TIMES AND THAT OF THE EGYPTIANS ONCE. IN **11** OF THESE **19** OCCURRENCES IT IS SAID THAT THE LORD DID THE HARDENING! **5** TIMES IT IS NOT DISTINGUISHED WHO DID THE HARDENING. **ONLY IN 3 VERSES DOES IT SAY THAT PHARAOH HARDENED HIS OWN HEART!** NOT ONLY IS THE DECLARATION OF THE LORD'S HAVING SOVEREIGNLY HARDENED PHARAOH'S HEART MADE **3** TIMES MORE OFTEN THAN IT IS SAID OF PHARAOH'S HARDENING HIS OWN HEART, BUT THE FORMER IS STATED **3** TIMES (EX. 4:21; 7:3, 13) BEFORE THE LATTER IS STATED ONCE! (7:14) LET THE OBJECTOR TO SOVEREIGN HARDENING EXPLAIN THE DIVINE ORDER and EMPHASIS OF THESE OCCURRENCES! (ROMANS 9:17+18!)

FANNY CROSBY (1820-1915)

ONE OF THE MOST PROLIFIC HYMN-WRITERS IN HISTORY — OVER 8,500 — WAS **THE FIRST WOMAN IN AMERICAN HISTORY TO ADDRESS THE JOINT SESSION of CONGRESS!**

SHE WAS A LIFELONG FRIEND OF PRESIDENT GROVER CLEVELAND!

DID YOU KNOW? by Eddie Eddings

DID YOU KNOW?

Andrew WAS BOUND TO A CROSS, WHERE HE PREACHED TO HIS PERSECUTORS UNTIL HE DIED.

C.S. LEWIS and PRESIDENT JOHN F. KENNEDY DIED ON NOVEMBER 22, 1963.

IT IS AGAINST THE LAW TO READ THE BIBLE ALOUD IN AN AMERICAN PUBLIC SCHOOL!

DID YOU KNOW?

VANCE HAVNER QUOTES:

"IT IS NOT UNCHRISTIAN TO OPPOSE HERESY. IT IS UNCHRISTIAN NOT TO OPPOSE IT."

"ACCORDING TO THE MODERN POLICY OF SWEETNESS AND LIGHT, OUR LORD SHOULD NEVER HAVE DENOUNCED THE PHARISEES. PAUL WOULD NEVER HAVE DIFFERED WITH PETER AT ANTIOCH. PAGE AFTER PAGE OF THE NEW TESTAMENT WOULD NEVER HAVE BEEN WRITTEN, NOR WOULD MARTIN LUTHER HAVE EVER DISTURBED THE STATUS QUO OF ROMANISM."

"DON'T BE A FIFTH-AMENDMENT CHRISTIAN!"

Eddie Eddings

"THE NIGHT WAS LONG; AND THE SHADOWS SPREAD
AS FAR AS THE EYE COULD SEE;
I STRETCHED MY HANDS TO A HUMAN CHRIST,
AND HE WALKED THROUGH THE DARK WITH ME.

OUT OF THE DIMNESS AT LAST WE CAME,
OUR FEET ON THE DAWN-WARMED SOD;
AND I SAW BY THE LIGHT OF HIS WONDROUS EYES
I WALKED WITH THE SON OF GOD."

—H.W. BEECHER

Did You Know?
by Eddie Eddings

FRANCES RIDLEY HAVERGAL (1836-1879) WAS A GENIUS! SHE COULD READ AT AGE 3, KNEW 7 LANGUAGES, MEMORIZED THE NEW TESTAMENT AS WELL AS THE PSALMS, ISAIAH, and THE MINOR PROPHETS. EXCELLING IN MUSIC, SHE SANG BEAUTIFULLY, COMPOSED, and COULD PLAY MUCH OF THE GREAT MASTERS' WORKS ON THE PIANO FROM MEMORY! SHE NEVER MARRIED, WAS OFTEN ILL, and DIED AT 42. SHE WROTE "LIKE A RIVER GLORIOUS," "WHO IS ON THE LORD'S SIDE?", AND MANY OTHERS.

DID YOU KNOW? by Eddie Eddings

DID YOU KNOW?

THE FIRST AMERICAN SERMON PRINTED WAS "THE SIN AND DANGER OF SELF-LOVE," A DISCOURSE "BASED ON THE TEXT FROM I CORINTHIANS 10:24. IT WAS DELIVERED DECEMBER 9, 1621, BY ROBERT CUSHMAN IN PLYMOUTH, MASSACHUSETTS, AND WAS FIRST PRINTED IN LONDON, ENGLAND IN 1622! IT WAS REPRINTED IN BOSTON, MASSACHUSETTS IN 1724!

Philip
HANGED UP AGAINST A PILLAR AT HIERAPOLIS IN PHRYGIA.

by Eddie Eddings

DID YOU KNOW?

NOTE WHAT THE LORD JESUS CHRIST SAID IN JOHN 10:26:

"BUT YOU DO NOT BELIEVE, BECAUSE YOU ARE NOT OF MY SHEEP." THE GREAT SHEPHERD DID NOT SAY... "YOU ARE NOT MY SHEEP BECAUSE YOU DO NOT BELIEVE!"—WHICH IS A VERY DIFFERENT THING!

"...I LAY DOWN MY LIFE FOR THE SHEEP."
—THE WORDS OF JESUS IN JOHN 10:15b

by Eddie Eddings

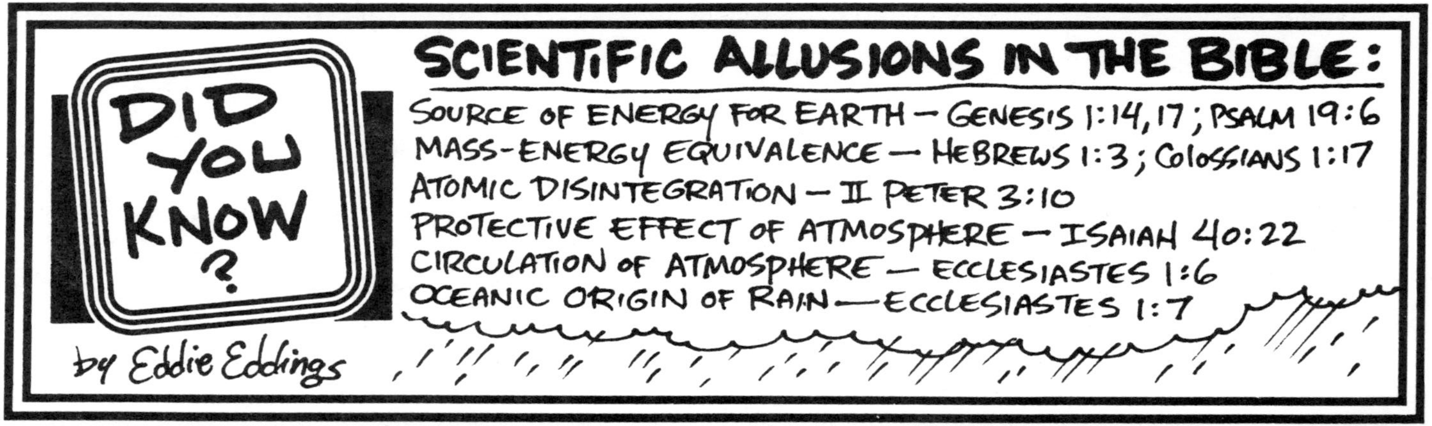

DID YOU KNOW?

SCIENTIFIC ALLUSIONS IN THE BIBLE:

- Source of Energy for Earth — Genesis 1:14,17; Psalm 19:6
- Mass-Energy Equivalence — Hebrews 1:3; Colossians 1:17
- Atomic Disintegration — II Peter 3:10
- Protective Effect of Atmosphere — Isaiah 40:22
- Circulation of Atmosphere — Ecclesiastes 1:6
- Oceanic Origin of Rain — Ecclesiastes 1:7

by Eddie Eddings

DID YOU KNOW?

There are TWO ACCOUNTS of BOOK-BURNING IN THE BIBLE! The first was by a wicked king who wanted to destroy the Word of God! (Jeremiah 36:23)

The second was by new converts to Christ who had once practiced sorcery! (Acts 19:18+19)

THERE ARE **14** NON-BIBLICAL BOOKS MENTIONED IN THE BIBLE!

Eddie Eddings

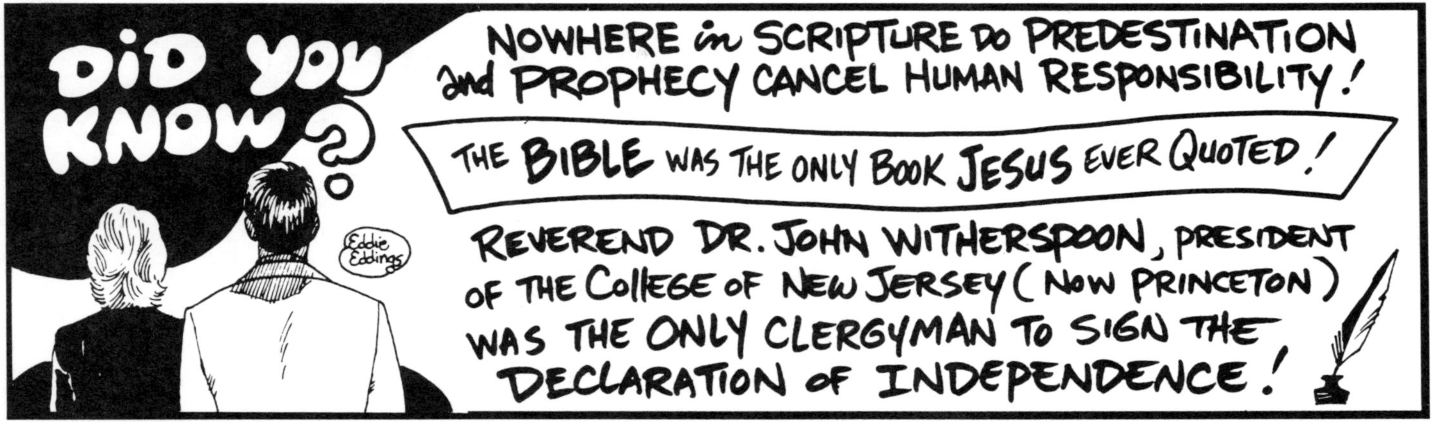

DID YOU KNOW?

Nowhere in Scripture do predestination and prophecy cancel human responsibility!

The BIBLE was the only book Jesus ever quoted!

Reverend Dr. John Witherspoon, president of the College of New Jersey (now Princeton) was the only clergyman to sign the Declaration of Independence!

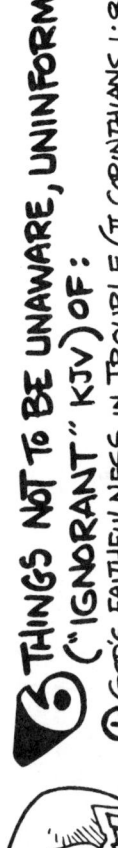

DID YOU KNOW?

6 things not to be unaware, uninformed ("ignorant" KJV) of:

1. God's faithfulness in trouble (II Corinthians 1:8-10)
2. Gospel responsibility (Romans 1:11-18)
3. Spiritual gifts (I Corinthians 12)
4. God's purpose for Israel (Romans 11:25-32)
5. The resurrection and future life (I Thessalonians 14:13-18)
6. God's judgments on backsliders (I Corinthians 10:1-13)

Well? Don't just sit there! Look up these verses!

DID YOU KNOW?
by Eddie Eddings

AUGUSTINE WELL SAID:
"Damnation is rendered to the wicked as a matter of debt, justice and desert, whereas the grace given to those who are delivered is free and unmerited, so that the condemned sinner cannot allege that he is unworthy of his punishment, nor the saint vaunt or boast as if he were worthy of his reward. Thus, in the whole course of this procedure there is no respect of persons. They who are condemned and they who are set at liberty constituted originally one and the same lump, equally infected with sin and liable to vengeance. Hence the justified may learn from the condemnation of the rest that that would have been their own punishment had not God's grace stepped in to their rescue."

DID YOU KNOW?
by Eddie Eddings

"THE LORD HAS ESTABLISHED HIS THRONE IN THE HEAVENS; AND HIS SOVEREIGNTY RULES OVER ALL."

(PSALM 103:19 NASB)

JOSEPHUS, THE JEWISH HISTORIAN, AND JEWISH TRADITION IDENTIFIES NAAMAN AS THE MAN WHO DREW HIS BOW AT RANDOM AND KILLED AHAB. (I KINGS 22:30-35)

DID YOU KNOW?

By Eddie Eddings

There is a best-selling Christian book that was **NEVER Completely Read By Anyone Except The Author!**

It is entitled "Cruden's Concordance of the Bible."

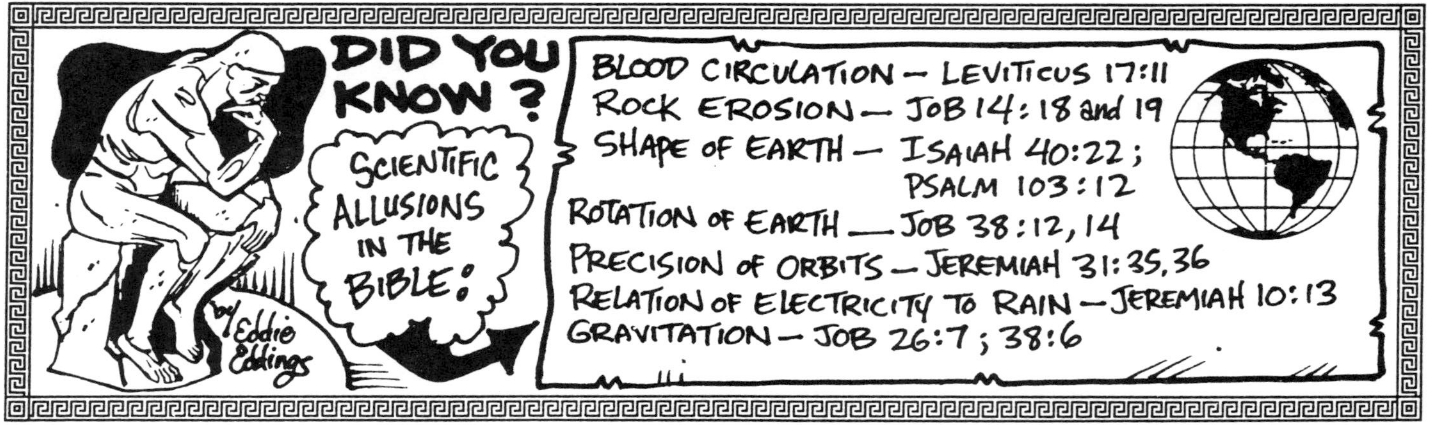

Thaddaeus — SHOT TO DEATH WITH ARROWS

"As long as error exists there must be controversy."

DID YOU KNOW?

Scientific Allusions in the Bible:

Blood Circulation — Leviticus 17:11
Rock Erosion — Job 14:18 and 19
Shape of Earth — Isaiah 40:22; Psalm 103:12
Rotation of Earth — Job 38:12,14
Precision of Orbits — Jeremiah 31:35,36
Relation of Electricity to Rain — Jeremiah 10:13
Gravitation — Job 26:7; 38:6

by Eddie Eddings

DID YOU KNOW? by Eddie Eddings

COTTON MATHER (1663-1728) RECEIVED HIS BACHELOR OF ARTS AT AGE **15**; HIS MASTER OF ARTS AT THE AGE OF **18**!

THE BOOK MOST READ IN ITS ORIGINAL NON-ENGLISH LANGUAGE IS THE GREEK NEW TESTAMENT.

James — BEHEADED AT JERUSALEM BY HEROD — A.D. 44 (?)

DID YOU KNOW? by Eddie Eddings

CHARLES WESLEY (1707-1788) WROTE **8,989** HYMNS! HE PENNED SOME WHILE ON HORSEBACK! HE WAS ONE OF THE MOST TALENTED POETS IN HISTORY — HE OFTEN WROTE LETTERS and SERMONS IN VERSE AND EVEN **SPOKE** IN **RHYME** ON SOME OCCASIONS!

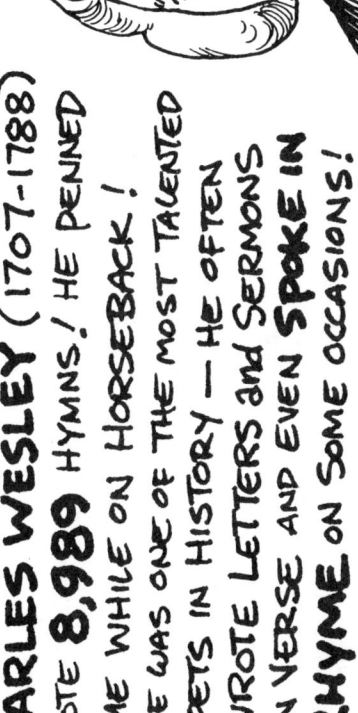

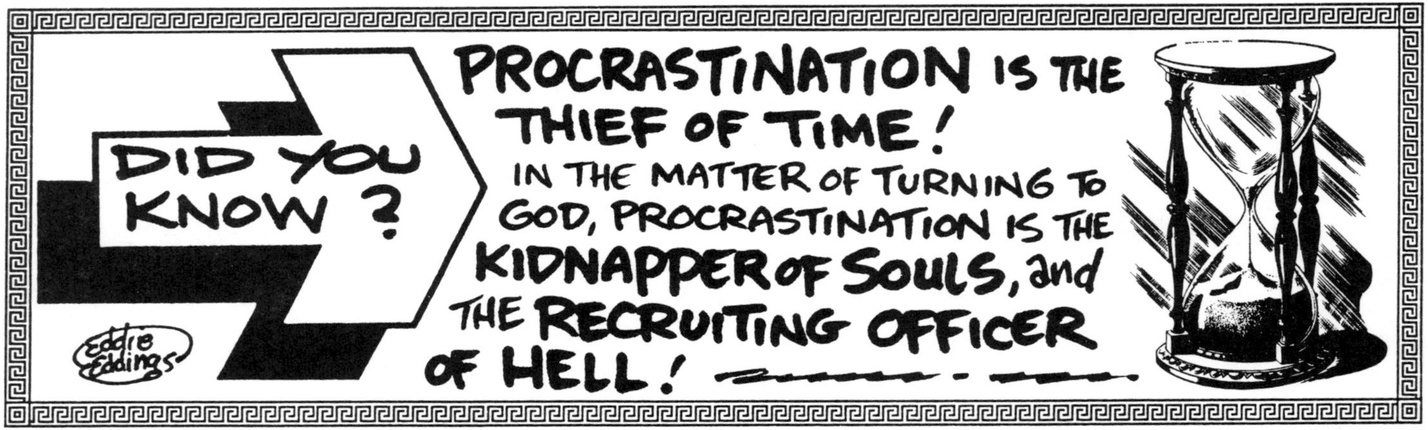

DID YOU KNOW?

PROCRASTINATION IS THE THIEF OF TIME!

IN THE MATTER OF TURNING TO GOD, PROCRASTINATION IS THE KIDNAPPER OF SOULS, and THE RECRUITING OFFICER OF HELL!

— Eddie Eddings

DID YOU KNOW

Bartholomew — FLAYED TO DEATH. JEROME SAYS HE WROTE A GOSPEL.

NO TOMBSTONE MARKS THE PLACE WHERE JOHN CALVIN IS BURIED!

by EDDIE EDDINGS

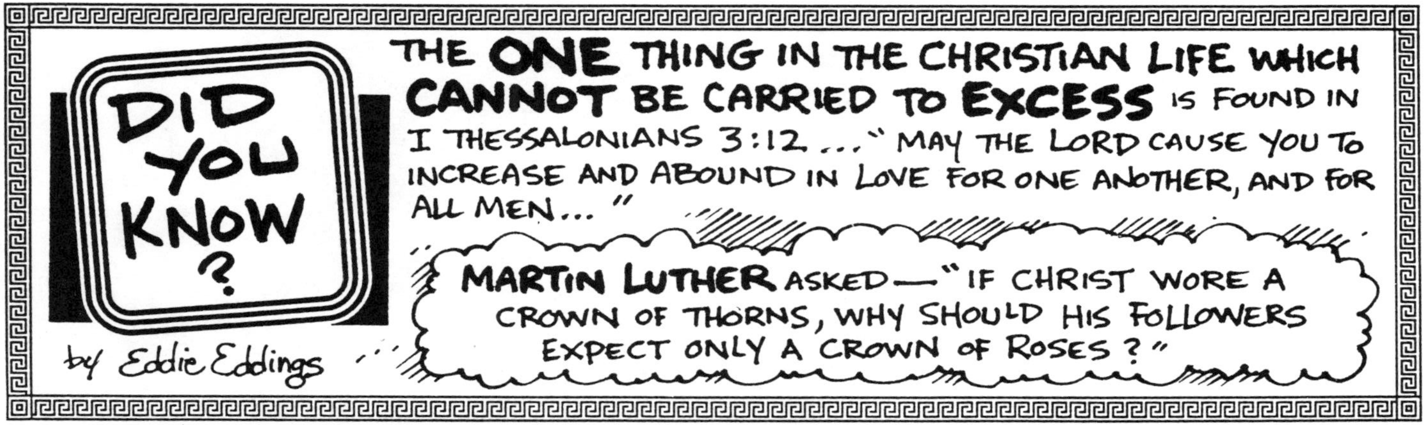

DID YOU KNOW?
by Eddie Eddings

THE **ONE** THING IN THE CHRISTIAN LIFE WHICH **CANNOT** BE CARRIED TO **EXCESS** IS FOUND IN I THESSALONIANS 3:12... "MAY THE LORD CAUSE YOU TO INCREASE AND ABOUND IN LOVE FOR ONE ANOTHER, AND FOR ALL MEN..."

MARTIN LUTHER ASKED — "IF CHRIST WORE A CROWN OF THORNS, WHY SHOULD HIS FOLLOWERS EXPECT ONLY A CROWN OF ROSES?"

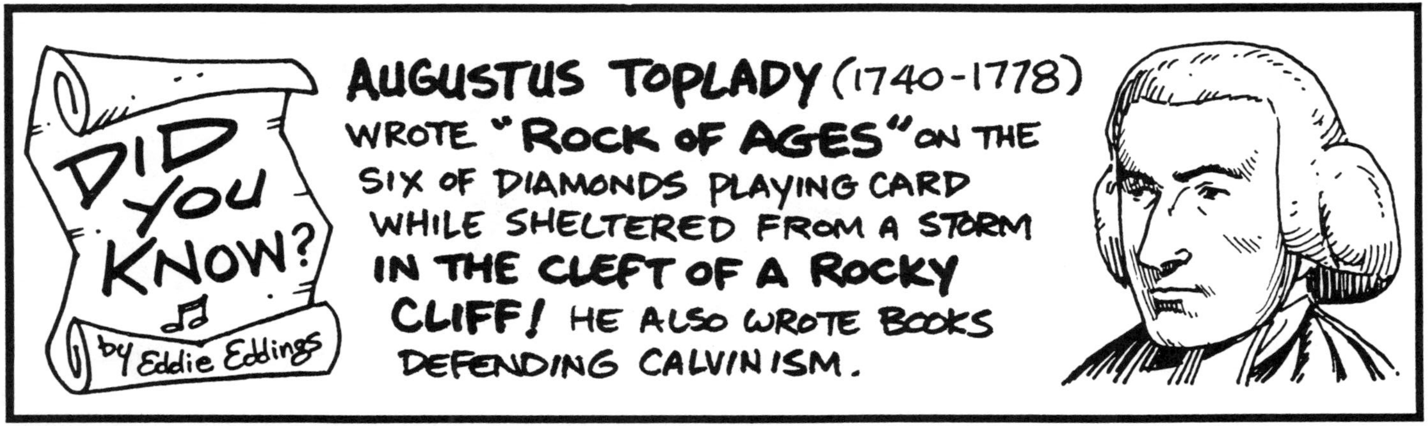

DID YOU KNOW?
by Eddie Eddings

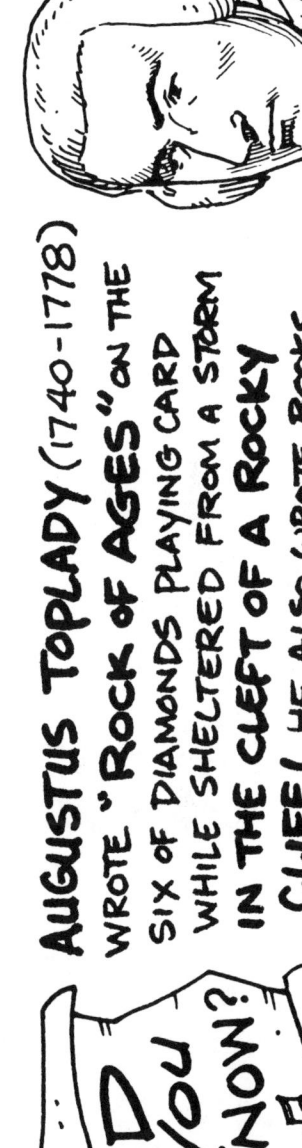

AUGUSTUS TOPLADY (1740-1778) WROTE "ROCK OF AGES" ON THE SIX OF DIAMONDS PLAYING CARD WHILE SHELTERED FROM A STORM **IN THE CLEFT OF A ROCKY CLIFF!** HE ALSO WROTE BOOKS DEFENDING CALVINISM.

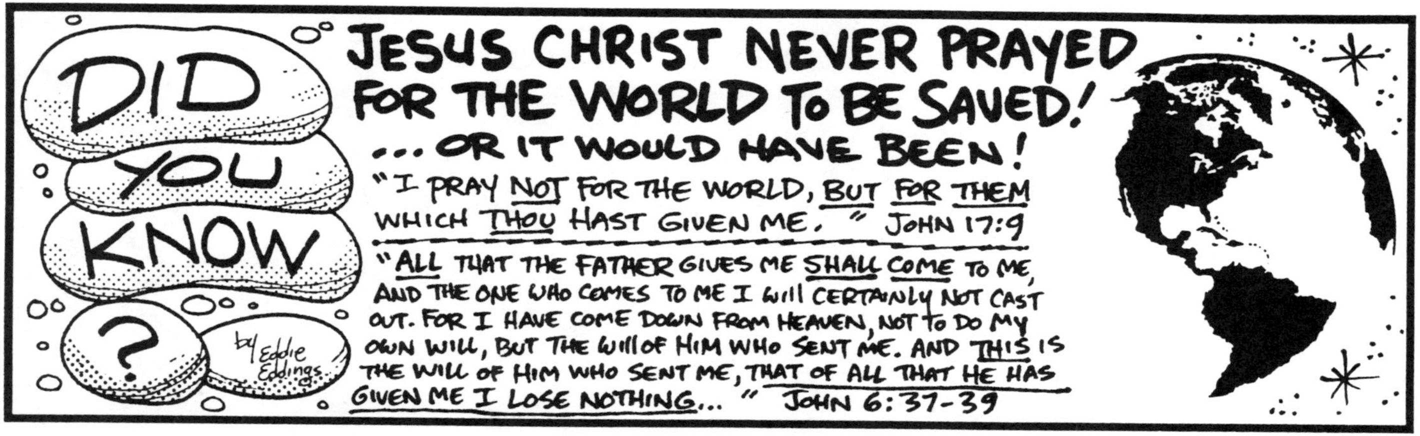

DID YOU KNOW?
by Eddie Eilers

JESUS CHRIST NEVER PRAYED FOR THE WORLD TO BE SAVED!
...OR IT WOULD HAVE BEEN!

"I PRAY NOT FOR THE WORLD, BUT FOR THEM WHICH THOU HAST GIVEN ME," JOHN 17:9

"ALL THAT THE FATHER GIVES ME SHALL COME TO ME, AND THE ONE WHO COMES TO ME I WILL CERTAINLY NOT CAST OUT. FOR I HAVE COME DOWN FROM HEAVEN, NOT TO DO MY OWN WILL, BUT THE WILL OF HIM WHO SENT ME. AND THIS IS THE WILL OF HIM WHO SENT ME, THAT OF ALL THAT HE HAS GIVEN ME I LOSE NOTHING..." JOHN 6:37-39

DID YOU KNOW?
by Eddie Eilers

THE FIRST BOOK FOR THE BLIND
WAS THE GOSPEL OF ST. MARK, PUBLISHED IN 1833!

D.L. MOODY READ EVERYTHING C.H. SPURGEON HAD IN PRINT, AND CONTINUED TO DO SO ALL HIS LIFE.

THERE ARE 3,037 MALE NAMES IN THE BIBLE and ONLY 181 FEMALE NAMES.

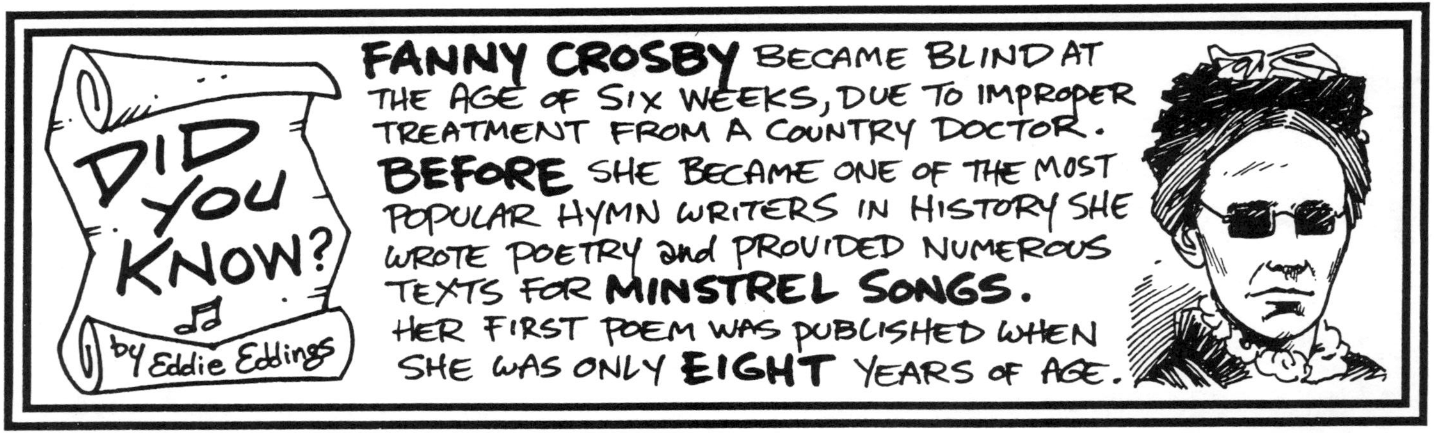

DID YOU KNOW?
by Eddie Edlings

FANNY CROSBY BECAME BLIND AT THE AGE OF SIX WEEKS, DUE TO IMPROPER TREATMENT FROM A COUNTRY DOCTOR. **BEFORE** SHE BECAME ONE OF THE MOST POPULAR HYMN WRITERS IN HISTORY, SHE WROTE POETRY and PROVIDED NUMEROUS TEXTS FOR **MINSTREL SONGS**. HER FIRST POEM WAS PUBLISHED WHEN SHE WAS ONLY **EIGHT YEARS OF AGE**.

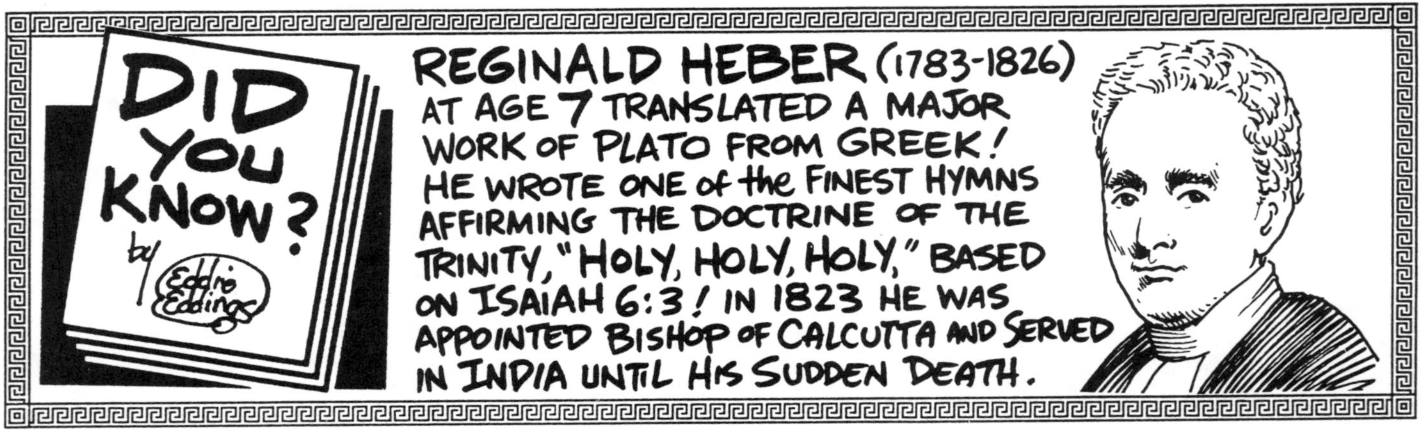

DID YOU KNOW?
by Eddie Edlings

REGINALD HEBER (1783-1826) AT AGE 7 TRANSLATED A MAJOR WORK OF PLATO FROM GREEK! HE WROTE ONE OF THE FINEST HYMNS AFFIRMING THE DOCTRINE OF THE TRINITY, "HOLY, HOLY, HOLY," BASED ON ISAIAH 6:3! IN 1823 HE WAS APPOINTED BISHOP OF CALCUTTA AND SERVED IN INDIA UNTIL HIS SUDDEN DEATH.

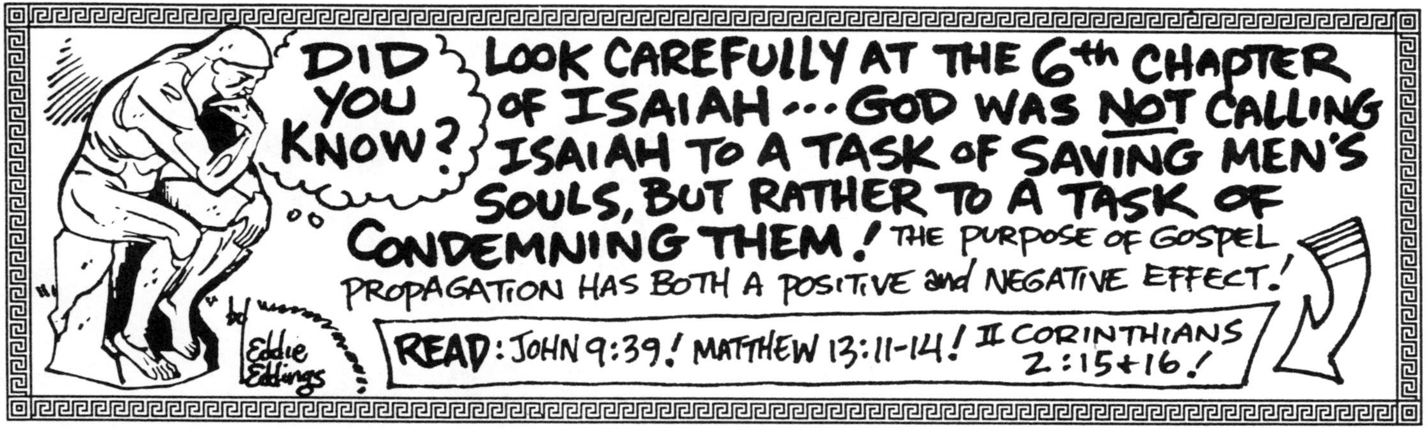

DID YOU KNOW? Look carefully at the 6th chapter of Isaiah... God was NOT calling Isaiah to a task of saving men's souls, but rather to a task of CONDEMNING THEM! The purpose of Gospel propagation has both a positive and negative effect.

READ: John 9:39! Matthew 13:11-14! II Corinthians 2:15+16!

— Eddie Eddings

Simon the Zealot

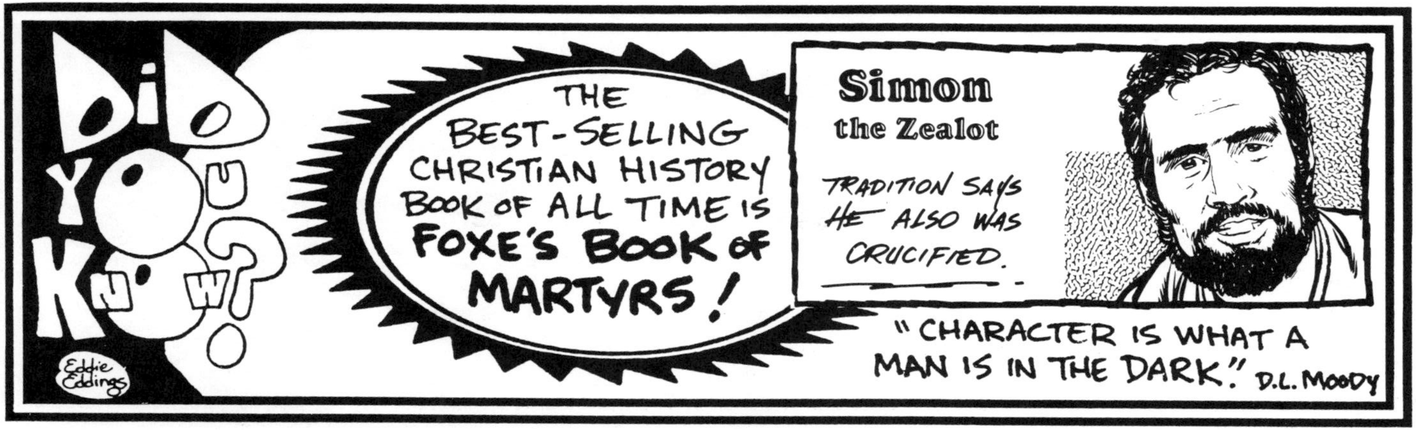

Tradition says he was also crucified.

"Character is what a man is in the dark." — D.L. Moody

THE BEST-SELLING CHRISTIAN HISTORY BOOK OF ALL TIME IS FOXE'S BOOK OF MARTYRS!

DID YOU KNOW?

— Eddie Eddings

DID YOU KNOW? by Eddie Eddings

"Nowadays we are expected to get along with everything and everybody, including the devil himself. It is the era of the oblique, the age of indirection, and we cultivate the 'art of almost saying something.'"

"One may be as straight as a gun barrel theologically and as empty as a gun barrel spiritually."

— VANCE HAVNER.

DID YOU KNOW? by Eddie Eddings

THOMAS KEN, (1637-1711) one of the most famous bishops of all time, was **IMPRISONED IN THE TOWER OF LONDON** for not supporting the King's ovations to Roman Catholicism. Thomas Ken wrote the hymn that is sung more often than **ANY OTHER IN THE WORLD**: "**THE DOXOLOGY**."

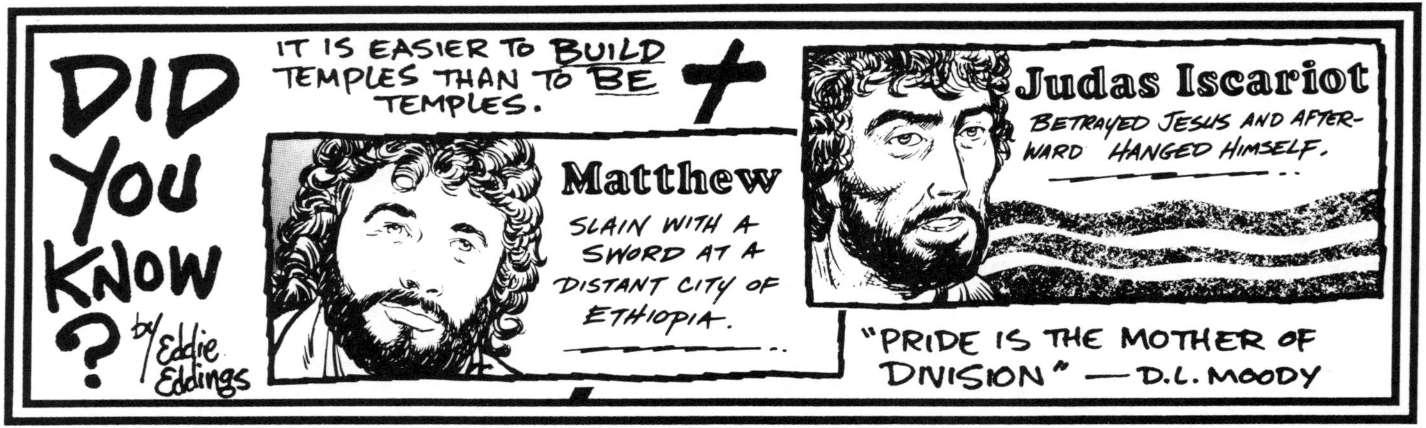

DID YOU KNOW?
by Eddie Eddings

Judas Iscariot — Betrayed Jesus and afterward hanged himself.

Matthew — Slain with a sword at a distant city of Ethiopia.

"PRIDE IS THE MOTHER OF DIVISION." —D.L. MOODY

IT IS EASIER TO BUILD TEMPLES THAN TO BE TEMPLES.

DID YOU KNOW?
by Eddie Eddings

PHILIP PAUL BLISS (1838-1876) Born in a log cabin. Left home at age of 11. Converted at age 12. Became a singing evangelist at the persistent encouragement of D.L. Moody. Wrote "Wonderful Words of Life," "Once for All," "Hallelujah! What a Savior!" "Jesus Loves Even Me," "I Will Sing of My Redeemer." He wrote the tune to "It Is Well With My Soul." Died when he re-entered a burning train to rescue his wife.

DID YOU KNOW?
by Eddie Eddings

A FLOATING CHURCH WAS CONSTRUCTED IN 1843 and MOORED IN THE EAST RIVER AT THE FOOT OF PIKE STREET, NEW YORK CITY. IT WAS KNOWN AS **THE FLOATING CHURCH OF OUR SAVIOUR!**

IT WAS ORGANIZED BY THE YOUNG MEN'S CHURCH MISSIONARY SOCIETY.

A YOUNG ARTIST NAMED **VINCENT VAN GOGH** PREACHED **SPURGEON'S SERMONS** IN LONDON'S GHETTOS!

GOD HATES:
- HOMOSEXUAL ACTS (LEVITICUS 18:22)
- DIVINATION (DEUTERONOMY 18:10)
- A PROUD LOOK (PROVERBS 6:16,17)
- DIVORCE (MALACHI 2:14-16)
- THOSE WHO LOVE VIOLENCE (PSALM 11:5)
- IDOLATRY (JEREMIAH 44:2-4)
- ANYONE WHO SOWS DISCORD AMONG BRETHREN (PROVERBS 6:19)

DID YOU KNOW?
by Eddie Eddings

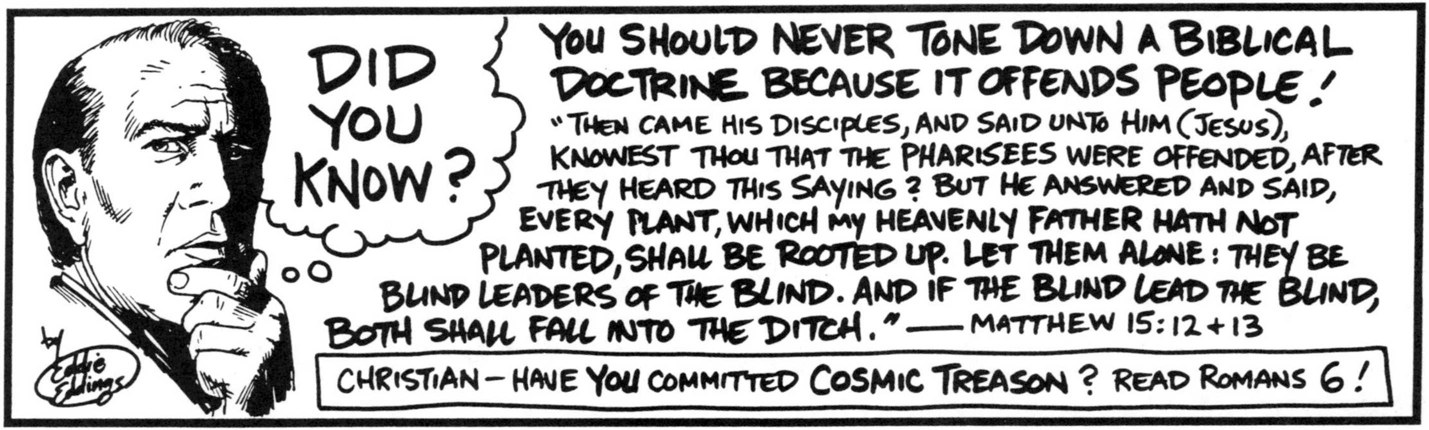

DID YOU KNOW?

You should never tone down a biblical doctrine because it offends people!

"Then came his disciples, and said unto him (Jesus), Knowest thou that the Pharisees were offended, after they heard this saying? But he answered and said, Every plant, which my heavenly Father hath not planted, shall be rooted up. Let them alone: they be blind leaders of the blind. And if the blind lead the blind, both shall fall into the ditch." — Matthew 15:12+13

CHRISTIAN — HAVE YOU COMMITTED COSMIC TREASON? READ ROMANS 6!

by Eddie Eddings

DID YOU KNOW?

"Go for souls — and go for the worst!" — William Booth

"Jesus was the most disturbing person in history." — Vance Havner

"Where death finds you, eternity binds you!"

"Trust God even when the pieces don't seem to fit." — Jim Harless

"Those who deny election deny that God can have mercy." — Robert Murray M'Cheyne

by Eddie Eddings

DID YOU KNOW?
by Eddie Eddings

VANCE HAVNER

"THE GOSPEL IS FOR LIFEBOATS NOT SHOWBOATS, AND A MAN MUST MAKE UP HIS MIND WHICH HE IS GOING TO OPERATE."

"TOO MANY CHURCH MEMBERS ARE STARCHED AND IRONED BUT NOT WASHED!"

"THE WORD OF GOD IS EITHER ABSOLUTE OR OBSOLETE."

DID YOU KNOW?
by Eddie Eddings

THE **FIRST** NATIONAL GOSPEL TRACT ORGANIZATION WAS THE AMERICAN TRACT SOCIETY, ESTABLISHED MAY 11, 1825, IN NEW YORK CITY. THEY HAVE SINCE MOVED THEIR HEADQUARTERS TO GARLAND, TEXAS WHERE THEY CONTINUE TO PUBLISH TRACTS AND GOSPEL COLORING BOOKS FOR KIDS!

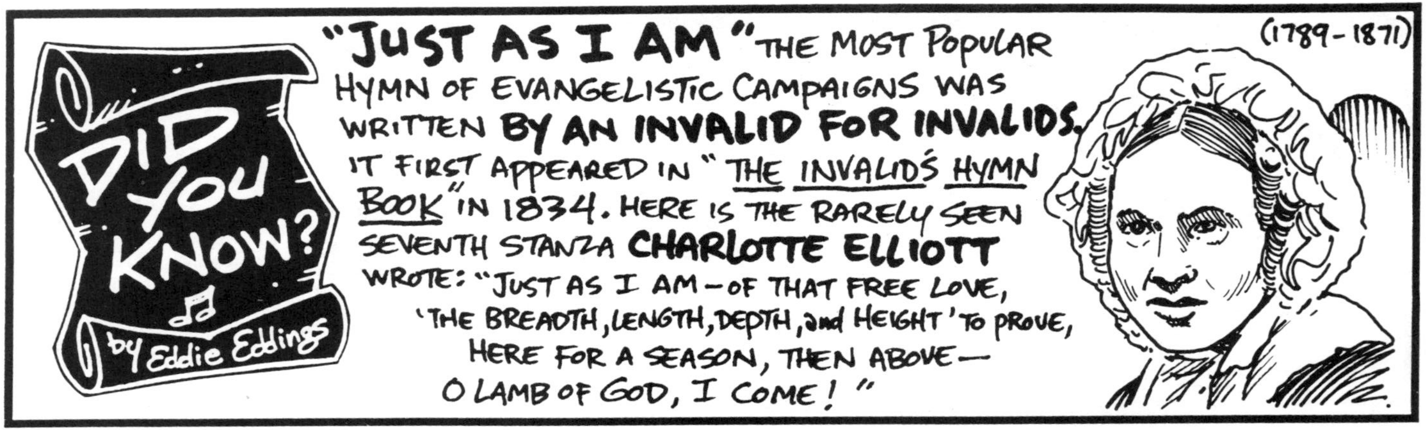

Did You Know? by Eddie Eddings

"JUST AS I AM" the most popular hymn of evangelistic campaigns was written **BY AN INVALID FOR INVALIDS.**

(1789–1871)

It first appeared in "THE INVALID'S HYMN BOOK" in 1834. Here is the rarely seen seventh stanza CHARLOTTE ELLIOTT wrote: "Just as I am – of that free love, the breadth, length, depth, and height, to prove, here for a season, then above —

O LAMB OF GOD, I COME!"

Did You Know? by Eddie Eddings

PREDESTINATION IS MUCH EASIER TO UNDERSTAND THAN THE DOCTRINE OF THE TRINITY! The real problem is that the natural man does not like it!

Our deeply entrenched mind-sets must give way to what God says about the matter.

Did You Know? by Eddie Eddings

FANNY CROSBY (1820-1915)—

The Methodist hymn writer, began to write texts for gospel songs when she was **45 YEARS OLD!**

She produced three hymns a week for an indefinite period of time using more than **200** pseudonyms in signing her lyrics. All of her songs were written from her Braille writer.

Did You Know?? by Eddie Eddings

Thomas was run through the body with a lance at Coromandel in the East Indies.

Not a leaf moves on the trees unless the Lord Himself doth please.

"If a man gets drunk and goes out and breaks his leg, so that it must be amputated, God will forgive him if he asks it, but he will have to hop around on one leg all his life." —D.L. Moody

Bible Quizzes

BIBLE QUIZ by Eddie Eddings
ANAGRAMS!

Anagrams are words or phrases that are scrambled to make other words or phrases. Example:

_____ RON HAD HER OLD SPACE GUNS
(CHARLES HADDON SPURGEON)

Unscramble this phrase for the name of a famous preacher or teacher:

OH CARL SELLS WIND

ANSWER: CHARLES SWINDOLL

BIBLE QUIZ by Eddie Eddings
ANAGRAMS!

Anagrams are words or phrases that are scrambled to make other words or phrases. Example:

_____ RON HAD HER OLD SPACE GUNS
(CHARLES HADDON SPURGEON)

Unscramble this phrase for the name of a famous preacher or teacher:

CLEANS R SCHOOL

ANSWER: CHARLES COLSON

BIBLE QUIZ by Eddie Eddings

ANAGRAMS!

Anagrams are words or phrases that are scrambled to make other words or phrases. Example:
— Ron had her old space guns — (Charles Haddon Spurgeon)

Unscramble this phrase for the name of a famous preacher or teacher:

JACK RIPE

ANSWER: J.I. PACKER

BIBLE QUIZ by Eddie Eddings

ANAGRAMS!

Anagrams are words or phrases that are scrambled to make other words or phrases. Example:
— Ron had her old space guns — (Charles Haddon Spurgeon)

Unscramble this phrase for the name of a famous preacher or teacher:

JANET HAD NO DRAWS

ANSWER: JONATHAN EDWARDS

BIBLE QUIZ by Eddie Eddings
ANAGRAMS!

Anagrams are words or phrases that are scrambled to make other words or phrases. Example:

— Ron had her old space guns — (Charles Haddon Spurgeon)

Unscramble this phrase for the name of a famous preacher or teacher:

No Joy Mrs. D.L. Tyndale

ANSWER: D. MARTYN LLOYD-JONES

BIBLE QUIZ by Eddie Eddings
ANAGRAMS!

Anagrams are words or phrases that are scrambled to make other words or phrases. Example:

— Ron had her old space guns — (Charles Haddon Spurgeon)

Unscramble this phrase for the name of a famous preacher or teacher:

Denny had rag or blouse

ANSWER: DONALD GREY BARNHOUSE

BIBLE QUIZ by Eddie Eddings

WHAT'S WRONG WITH THESE STATEMENTS?

① THE BIBLE SAYS THAT ELIJAH WAS TAKEN UP TO HEAVEN IN A CHARIOT OF FIRE.
② THE EPISTLES WERE THE WIVES OF THE APOSTLES.
③ SAUL OF TARSUS WAS CONVERTED ON THE JERICHO ROAD.
④ ABRAHAM WAS THE FIRST ISRAELITE.
⑤ JOHN SAID, "I WAS IN THE SPIRIT ON THE SABBATH DAY."

MAP OF LIFE — PRE-DESTINATION — DESTINATION

① HE "WENT UP BY A WHIRLWIND INTO HEAVEN." (II KINGS 2:11)
② LETTERS WRITTEN BY APOSTLES. ③ DAMASCUS ROAD.
④ JACOB'S (ISRAEL'S) CHILDREN WERE THE FIRST ISRAELITES.
⑥ "ON THE LORD'S DAY." (REV. 1:10)

BIBLE QUIZ by Eddie Eddings

ROCKS

① WHO DIED AND THE ROCKS BROKE?
② WHO WAS TOLD TO SPEAK TO A ROCK?
③ WHO WAS TOLD TO HIDE HIS GIRDLE IN THE HOLE OF A ROCK?
④ WHO OWNED THE SEPULCHER HEWN OUT OF A ROCK IN WHICH JESUS WAS BURIED?
⑤ WHO CARRIED 10,000 PEOPLE TO THE TOP OF A ROCK AND PUSHED THEM DOWN?

① JESUS (MATT. 27:51) ② MOSES (NUM. 20:7-8)
③ JEREMIAH (JER. 13:3-4) ④ JOSEPH OF ARIMATHAEA (MARK 15:46) ⑤ AMAZIAH (I CHRON. 25:11-12)

BIBLE QUIZ by Eddie Eddings

How many "F"s in the sentence below?

THE FOXES OF SAMSON DESTROYED THE CORNFIELDS OF THE PHILISTINES.

Answer: Four

BIBLE QUIZ by Eddie Eddings

ANAGRAMS!

Anagrams are words or phrases that are scrambled to make other words or phrases. Example:

— RON HAD HER OLD SPACE GUNS —
(CHARLES HADDON SPURGEON)

Unscramble this phrase for the name of a famous preacher or teacher:

RUN IT THERMAL

ANSWER: MARTIN LUTHER

Bible Quiz by Edie Eddings

What Bible woman was it whose name is not mentioned, whose death was different from any other ever recorded, whose body never saw corruption, and whose shroud was composed of a material which you find in every kitchen?

ANSWER: LOT'S WIFE

Bible Quiz by Edie Eddings

ANAGRAMS!

Anagrams are words or phrases that are scrambled to make other words or phrases. Example:

— Ron had her old space guns —
(CHARLES HADDON SPURGEON)

Unscramble this phrase for the name of a famous preacher or teacher:

TWO HID MY DOG.

ANSWER: DWIGHT MOODY

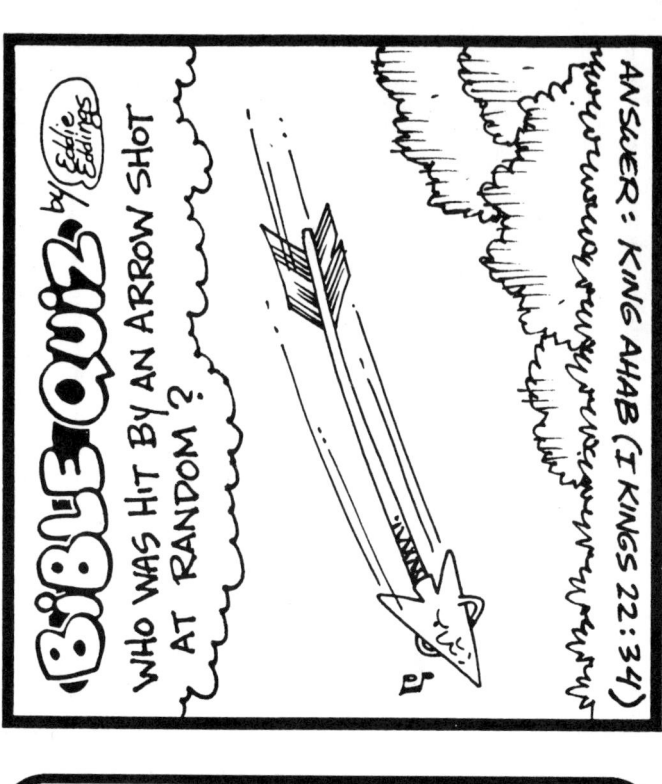
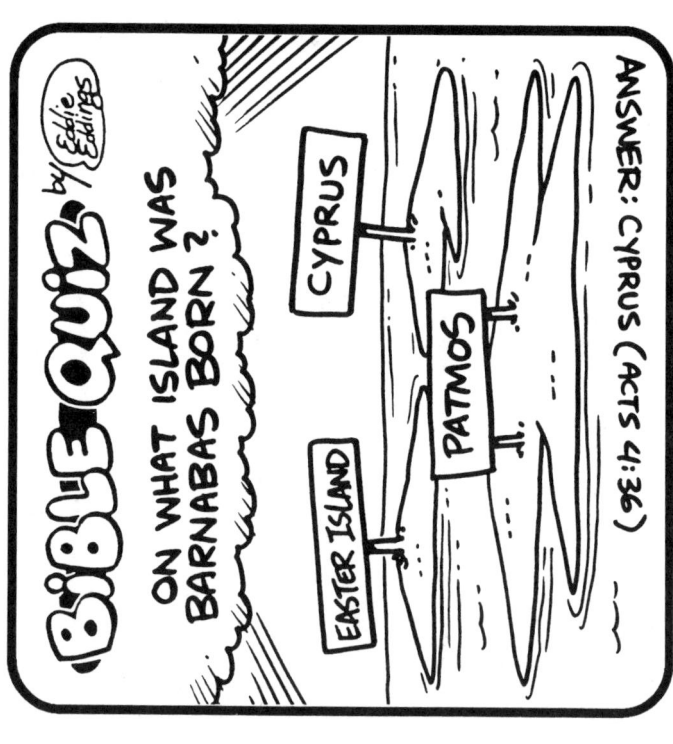

BIBLE QUIZ by Eddie Eddings

ANAGRAMS!

Anagrams are words or phrases that are scrambled to make other words or phrases. Example:

Ron had her old space guns —— (Charles Haddon Spurgeon)

Unscramble this phrase for the name of a famous preacher or teacher:

ANN... GOD'S PREACHER SHOULD.

ANSWER: CHARLES HADDON SPURGEON

BIBLE QUIZ by Eddie Eddings

ANAGRAMS!

Anagrams are words or phrases that are scrambled to make other words or phrases. Example:

Ron had her old space guns —— (Charles Haddon Spurgeon)

Unscramble this phrase for the name of a famous preacher or teacher:

O LIE, WE FIGHT GREED.

ANSWER: GEORGE WHITEFIELD

BIBLE QUIZ by Eddie Eddings

ANAGRAMS!

Anagrams are words or phrases that are scrambled to make other words or phrases. Example:

RON HAD HER OLD SPACE GUNS — (CHARLES HADDON SPURGEON)

Unscramble this phrase for the name of a famous preacher or teacher:

WANT THE RHYME

ANSWER: MATTHEW HENRY

BIBLE QUIZ by Eddie Eddings

Where is the first recorded law on kidnapping and what was the penalty for this crime?

"GUILTY AS SIN!"

ANSWER: EXODUS 21:16 — DEATH PENALTY

The Illustrated Spurgeon

"Ungodly men only need rope enough and they will hang themselves; their own iniquities shall be their punishment. Hell itself is but evil fully developed, torturing those in whom it dwells. Oh! Happy they who have fled to Jesus to find refuge from their former sins, such, and such only will escape."

"You have heard a great many Arminian **sermons**, I dare say; but you never heard an Arminian **prayer** – for the saints in prayer appear as one in word, and deed and mind. An Arminian on his knees would pray desperately like a Calvinist. He cannot pray about free will: there is no room for it."

"Christ is the A, and he is the Z of the salvation alphabet."

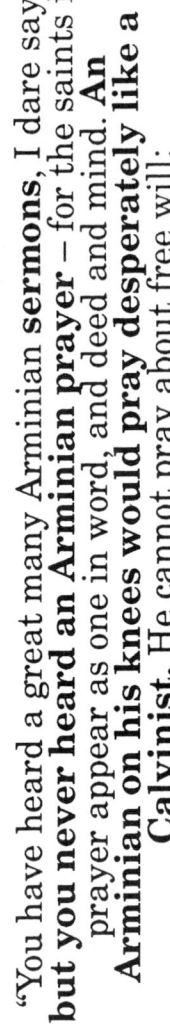

ON COMMENTARIES:

"A respectable acquaintance with the opinions of the [theological] giants of the past, might have saved many an erratic thinker from wild interpretations and outrageous inferences...**It seems odd, that certain men who talk so much of what the Holy Spirit reveals to themselves, should think so little of what He has revealed to others."**

C.H. Spurgeon

"You might as soon yoke a gnat with an archangel as think of your going in to help Christ save you. To join a filthy rag from off a dunghill with the golden garments of a king or a queen cannot be permitted. Christ will be everything, or else He will be nothing. You must be saved wholly by mercy, or else not at all. There must not be even a trace of the fingers of self-righteousness on the acts and documents of Divine Grace."

C.H. Spurgeon

"THINK LIGHTLY OF HELL, AND YOU WILL THINK LIGHTLY OF THE CROSS."

"You may laugh yourself into Hell, but you cannot laugh yourself out of it."

"Neglect of private prayer is the locust which devours the strength of the church."

"I suspect that every saved soul in Heaven is a great wonder, and that **Heaven is a vast museum of wonders of grace and mercy,** *a palace of miracles*, in which everything will surprise everyone who gets there."

C.H. Spurgeon

"I am not quite sure about a smile being a sin, and, at any rate, I think it less a crime to cause a momentary laughter than a half-hour's profound slumber."

"The man who wears his piety like a mask at a carnival, so that, when he gets home, he changes from a saint to a savage, from an angel to a devil, from John to Judas, from a benefactor to a bully, – such a man, I say, knows very well what formalism and hypocrisy can do for him, but he has no vestige of true religion. Fig trees do not bear figs on certain days, and thorns at other times; but they are true to their nature at all seasons."

"How can men say that the doctrine of distinguishing grace makes men careless about souls?.... Was Whitefield a man who cared nothing for the salvation of the people? He who flew like a seraph throughout England and America unceasingly proclaiming the grace of God, was he selfish? **Yet he was distinctly a free-grace preacher.** Did Jonathan Edwards have no concern for the souls of others? Oh, how he wept, and cried, and warned them of the wrath to come! **Time would fail me to tell of the lovers of men who have been lovers of the truth."**

C.H. Spurgeon's LAST WORDS at the Tabernacle:

"If you wear the livery of Christ, you will find Him so meek and lowly of heart, that you will find rest unto your souls. He is the most magnanimous of captains. There never was His like among the choicest of princes. He is always to be found in the thickest part of the battle. When the wind blows cold He always takes the bleak side of the hill. The heaviest end of the cross lies ever on His shoulders. If He bids us carry a burden, He carries it also. If there is any thing that is gracious, generous, kind, and tender, yea, lavish and superabundant in love, you always find it in Him. His service is life, peace, joy. Oh, that you would enter on it at once! God help you to enlist under the banner of JESUS CHRIST!"

"The **astronomer** cannot put the **stars in a row**, like a row of gas lights, to please you; and the **minister** cannot put **the doctrines into a shape** in which **you would wish to have them cast**. All the astronomer does is to **map them out**, and say, 'That is how they are in the sky.' *You must then look at the sky, and see whether it is so.* All I have to do is tell you what I find in the Bible; if you do not like it, remember, that is no refutation of it, nor do I care for your liking it or not liking it; **the only thing is,** *is it in the Bible?*"

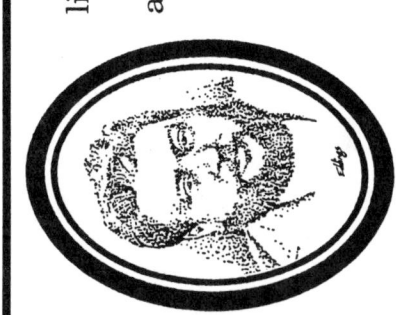

"THERE ARE SOME WHO, LIKE LYDIA, HAVE THEIR HEARTS OPENED NOT BY THE CROWBAR OF CONVICTION, BUT BY THE PICKLOCK OF DIVINE GRACE. SWEETLY DRAWN, ALMOST SILENTLY ENCHANTED BY THE LOVELINESS OF JESUS, THEY SAY, 'DRAW ME, AND I WILL RUN AFTER THEE.'"

"I ask the man who dares to say that Calvinism is a licentious religion, what he thinks of the character of Augustine, or Calvin, or Whitefield, who in successive ages were the exponents of the system of grace; or what will he say of the Puritans, whose works are full of them? *Had a man been an Arminian in those days, he would have been accounted the vilest heretic breathing, but now we are looked upon as the heretics, and they as the orthodox.*"

"I felt when I was coming up to preach tonight as if I had been down like a little child to the sea, and I had stooped to the wave and filled my palms as well as I could with the sparkling water, but as I have been coming to bring it to you, it has nearly all trickled away, *for I am not able to hold it by reason of my leaking hands.*"

C.H. Spurgeon

"There are many of our opponents, who, when they run short of matter, invent and make for themselves a man of straw, call that John Calvin, and then shoot all their arrows at it."

C.H. Spurgeon

"There are prayers that break the backs of words; they are too heavy for any human language to carry."

"As well might a gnat seek to drink in the ocean, as a finite creature to comprehend the Eternal God."

"It would also be unnecessary to repeat the whole of the 9th chapter of Romans. As long as that remains in the Bible no man shall be able to prove Arminianism."

"There are two sins of man that are bred in the bone, and that continually come out in the flesh. One is self-dependence and the other is self-exaltation."

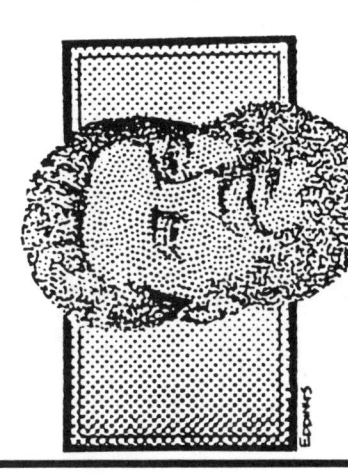

"And hear me distinctly again, lest any should mistake me. I always like to preach so that there can be no mistake about it. I do not want so to preach that you will say in the judgment of charity, he could not have meant what he said – that I do believe that none others were redeemed than those who are or shall be redeemed from the guilt, the punishment, and the power of sin, because I say again, *it is abhorrent to my reason, much less to my views of Scripture*, to conceive that the damned ever were redeemed, and that the lost in perdition were ever washed in the Saviour's blood, or that His blood was ever shed with an intention of saving them."

C.H. Spurgeon

"We believe in the perseverance of the saints, but many are not saints, and therefore do not persevere."

"Daniel opened his window towards Jerusalem, but we open our hearts towards Heaven."

"Oh, wretched man that I am," said the apostle Paul.... He said this, not because he was not a saint, but because he was so far advanced in the way of holiness."

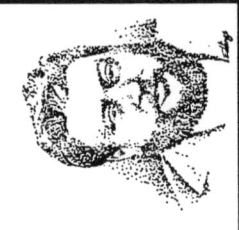

"I know, dear friends, there are some who are so afraid of the doctrine of election that the mention of it produces alarm. If they were to meet a lion in their way they would not be more terrified than they are when they see this doctrine in Scripture or hear it from the pulpit."

"If you feel you cannot repent, go to Him and tell Him so, for He is exalted to give repentance, as well as remission of sins."

"To every saved man, it is the greatest miracle of all that he is himself a believer."

"No man should give sleep to his eyes or slumber to his eyelids while he has a doubt about his eternal state."

"He that will not believe in Christ would murder God if he could."

— C. H. Spurgeon

"You must take all the Bible or none. It stands or falls together. He to whom it belongs will no more yield to its being divided, than the true mother, in Solomon's day, would consent to the dividing of the living child."

"If only one second ago I trusted the Savior I am safe; as the man who has believed in Jesus fifty years, and who has all that while walked uprightly."

— C. H. Spurgeon

"In the olden times our sires dealt sturdy blows against the forests of error, and labored hard to lay the ax at the root of the trees;
But, alas! Their sons appear to be quite as diligent to destroy the truth and to overthrow all that their fathers built up.
O for the good old times again! O for an hour of Luther's hatchet, or Calvin's mighty ax!"

"I know the Scripture says, '**No man can serve two masters.**' Now this is often misunderstood. Some read it, 'No man can *serve two* masters.' **Yes he can**; he can serve three or four. The way to read it is this: 'No man can serve two *masters*.'...He can serve two, but they cannot **both** be his master...He may live for **twenty** different purposes, but he cannot live for more than **one** master purpose — there can only be one master purpose in his soul."

"The hypocrite is content if his garments be washed; but the true suppliant cries, 'Wash me.'"

"All repetitions are not 'vain repetitions'! Souls in agony have no space to find variety of language; pain has to content itself with monotones."

"We are bound to tell you the truth, we are not bound to give you the power to understand it; and besides, this is not a subject for understanding, it is a matter for believing because it is revealed in the Word of God. It is one of the axioms of theology that, if man be lost, God must not be blamed for it; and it is also an axiom of theology that, if man be saved, God must have all the glory of it."

"No man will ever put on the robe of Christ's righteousness till he is stripped of his fig leaves, nor will he wash in the fount of mercy till he perceives his filthiness. Therefore, my brethen, we must not cease to declare the law, its demands, its threatenings, and the sinner's multiplied breaches of it."

"We had better far be inconsistent with ourselves than with the inspired Word. I have been called an Arminian Calvinist or a Calvinistic Arminian, and I am quite content so long as I can keep close to my Bible."

C.H. Spurgeon

"<u>Never</u> exalt one attribute at the expense of another. Let boundless mercy be seen in calm consistency with stern justice and unlimited sovereignty. **The true character of God is fitted to awe, impress, and humble the sinner:** <u>be careful not to misrepresent your Lord.</u>"

"Many a Jonah, who now rejects the doctrines of the grace of God, only needs to be put into the whale's belly and he will cry out with the soundest free-grace man, 'SALVATION IS OF THE LORD.'"

"I have often thought that if I had read in Scripture that 'if Charles Haddon Spurgeon shall call upon the name of the Lord, he shall be saved,' I would not have felt as sure of salvation as I do now, because I would have concluded that there might have been somebody else of that name, and I would have said, 'surely it did not mean me.' But when the Lord says, 'whosoever,' I cannot get out of that circle."

"When it [i.e. Calvinism] is preached there is a something in it which excites thought. A man may hear sermons upon the other theory which shall glance over him as the swallow's wing gently sweeps the brook, but these old doctrines either make a man so angry that he goes home and cannot sleep for very hatred, or else they bring him down into lowliness of thought, feeling the immensity if the things which he has heard.

Either way it excites and stirs him up not temporarily, but in a most lasting manner. These doctrines haunt him, he kicks against the pricks, and full often the Word forces a way into his soul. And I think this is no small thing for any doctrine to do, in an age given to slumber, and with human hearts so indifferent to the truth of God. *I know that many men have gained more good by being made angry under a sermon than by being pleased by it, for being angry they have turned the truth over and over again, and at last the truth has burned its way right into their hearts. They have played with edge-tools, but they have cut themselves at last.*"

"If an act of sin would increase my usefulness tenfold, I have no right to do it; and if an act of righteousness would appear likely to destroy all my apparent usefulness, I am yet to do it. It is yours and mine to do the right though the heavens fall, and follow the command of Christ whatever the consequences may be."

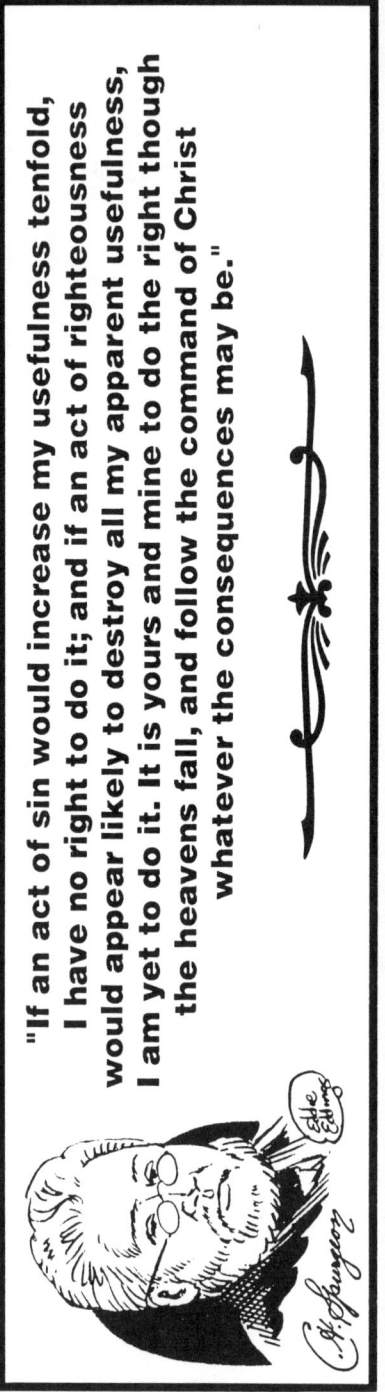

"Oh! What freeness was there in the gospel when Christ preached it! No cold theology froze His lips; words did not hang like icicles there, but *out of His mouth flowed rivers of living water*."

When **God** says to a sinner, '**Live**,' *all the devils in hell cannot keep him in the grave.* If the Lord should say to a blasphemer here today, '**Live**,' *that blasphemer **must** become a saint*."

"Finally, Christian, never give up any sinner. Never think that any man is beyond salvation. I charge you by the solemn thought that *God looketh for nothing in man, and saveth only according to the sweet counsels of His own will,* bring every man you meet with before God in prayer, plead with every man, preach Christ to every man, *tell every man that Christ can save,* tell that sinner that whatever there may not be in him, Christ's power is still the same, that His arm is not shortened neither is His ear heavy; and spread ye the glad news that *it is not of the will of man, nor blood, nor birth, but by the power of the Spirit of God according to the will of the Most High.*"

— C.H. Spurgeon

"The greatest missionaries that have ever lived have believed in God's choice of them; and instead of this doctrine leading to inaction, it has ever been an irresistible motive power, *and it will be so again.* It was the secret energy of the Reformation."

— C.H. Spurgeon

"The heart is like a dark cellar, full of lizards, cockroaches, beetles, and all kinds of reptiles and insects, which in the dark we see not. But the Law takes down the shutters and lets in the light, and we see the evil."

— C.H. Spurgeon

Charles Haddon Spurgeon

"The way to make strong Christians is to feed them well; let them have good spiritual food, and then we shall rear good, strong backboned Christians. We have got enough jelly-fish now."

"I am not a Calvinist by choice, but because I cannot help it."

"I did not ask whether you believe in Calvinism. It is possible you may not. But I believe you will before you enter heaven. I am persuaded that as God may have washed your hearts, He will wash your brains before you enter heaven."

C.H. Spurgeon's FIRST WORDS at the Tabernacle:

"I would propose that the subject of the ministry in this house, as long as this platform shall stand, and as long as this house shall be frequented by worshippers, shall be the person of JESUS CHRIST. I am never ashamed to avow myself a Calvinist; I do not hesitate to take the name of Baptist; but if I am asked what is my creed, I reply, 'It is Jesus Christ.' My venerated predecessor, Dr. Gill, has left a Body of Divinity, admirable and excellent in its way; but the Body of Divinity to which I would pin and bind myself forever, God helping me, is not his system, or any other human treatise; but Christ Jesus, who is the sum and substance of the Gospel, who is in Himself all theology, the incarnation of every precious truth, the all-glorious personal embodiment of the Way, the Truth, and the Life."

"We may seek God even when we have sinned. If sin could blockade the mercy-seat it would be all over for us, but the mercy is that there are gifts even for the rebellious, and an advocate for men who sin."

C.H. Spurgeon

"When preaching and private talk are not available, you have a tract ready, and this is often an effectual method. Some tracts would not convert a beetle: there is not enough in them to interest a fly. Get good striking tracts, or none at all. But a telling, touching gospel tract may often be the seed of eternal life; therefore, do not go out without your tracts."

"If there be a man before me who says that the wrath of God is too heavy a punishment for his little sin, I ask him, if the sin be little, why does he not give it up?"

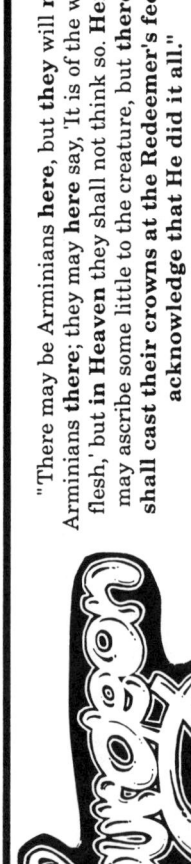

"There may be Arminians here, but they will not be Arminians there; they may here say, 'It is of the will of the flesh,' but in Heaven they shall not think so. Here they may ascribe some little to the creature, but there they shall cast their crowns at the Redeemer's feet, and acknowledge that He did it all."

"SALVATION IS OF THE LORD." – Jonah 2:9
"Jonah learned this sentence of good theology in a strange college."

"The basis and groundwork of Arminian theology lies in attaching *undue importance to man*, and *giving God rather the second place than the first*."

"TO WHOM IS RESERVED THE BLACKNESS OF DARKNESS FOR EVER." —JUDE 13
"Reserved' seats in Hell! DID YOU EVER THINK OF THAT?"

"It always seems inexplicable to me that those who claim free will so very boldly for man should not also allow some free will to God. *Why should not Jesus Christ have the right to choose His own bride?*"

"As long as a man is alive and out of Hell, he cannot have any cause to complain."

"Many of you will read a novel from beginning to end, **and what have you got? A mouthful of froth when you have done.** But you cannot read the Bible; that solid, lasting, substantial, and satisfying food goes uneaten, **locked up in the cupboard of neglect;** while anything that man writes, a catch of the day, is **greedily devoured**."

"You will find the Scriptures **enlarge** as you enter them; the **more** you study them the **less** you will appear to know of them, **for they widen out as we approach them.**"

"If, then, I find taught in one place that everything is fore-ordained, *that is true*; and if I find in another place that man is responsible for all his actions, *that is true*; and it is my folly that leads me to imagine that two truths can ever contradict each other. These two truths, I do not believe, can ever be welded into one upon any human anvil, but one they shall be in eternity: they are two lines that are so nearly parallel, that the mind that shall pursue them farthest, will never discover that they converge; but they do converge, and *they will meet somewhere in eternity, close to the throne of God, whence all truth doth spring.*"

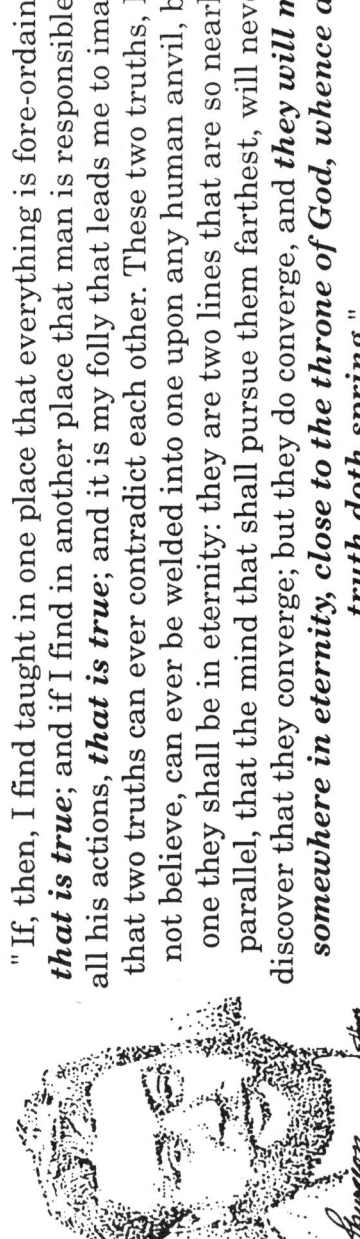

"Self-esteem is that speck in the eye which most effectually mars human vision; the Great Surgeon of souls removes this from us chiefly by sanctified afflictions...*Your trials have been the cleft of the rock in which God has set you as He did His servant Moses, that you might behold His glory as it passed by.*"

"We do not regulate our theology by the clock, but by eternal truth. We may not know what's o'clock in the Christian world, but we believe in 'Jesus Christ, the same yesterday, today, and forever.'"

"Maturity in grace makes us willing to part with worldly goods; the green apple needs a sharp twist to separate it from the bough; but the ripe fruit parts readily from the wood. Maturity in grace makes it easier to part with life itself; the unripe pear is scarcely beaten down with much labor, while its mellow companion drops readily into the hand with the slightest shake. Rest assured that love of the things of this life, and cleaving to this present state, are sure indications of immaturity in the divine life."

"On that day when Peter stood up with the eleven and charged the people that with wicked hands they had slain the Savior, three thousand of these persons who were thus justly accused of His crucifixion became believers in Him [Acts 2].

That was an answer to Jesus' prayer. ['Father, forgive them; for they know not what they do.'— Luke 23:34]"

— C.H. SPURGEON

C.H. Spurgeon

"Do you think to come to Jesus up the ladder of knowledge?

Come down, sir, you will meet him at the foot."

"Men will allow God to be everywhere except on His throne...But it is God upon the throne that we love to preach."

"I believe there is a deep, secret, essential, vital union between all the elect of God who have been quickened by the power of the Holy Spirit, and have been washed in the 'fountain filled with blood.'

Our differences of opinion upon some points are incidental to thoughtful humanity, and to truth, and we wake each other up — not always in the right spirit, perhaps, but our merciful God overrules it for the right."

C.H. Spurgeon

"The fact that conversion and salvation are of God, is a humbling truth. *It is because of its humbling character that men do not like it.* To be told that God must save me if I am saved, and that I am in His hand, as clay is in the hands of the potter, 'I do not like it' saith one. **Well, I thought you would not; whoever dreamed you would?"**

"What a blessing that in a world of uncertainties we have something sure to rest upon! We hasten from the quicksands of human speculations to the *terra firma* of Divine Revelation."

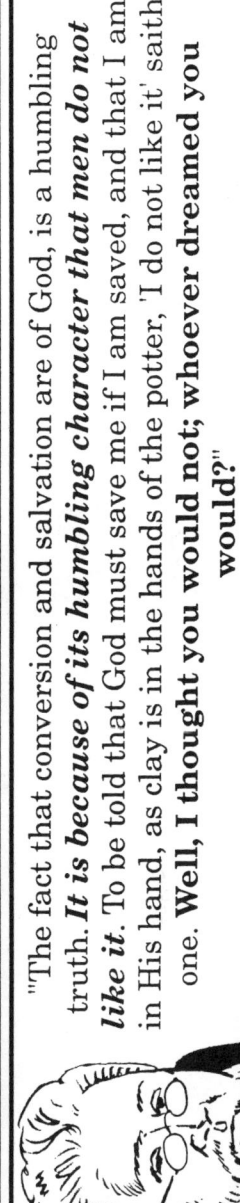

"Few preachers of religion do believe thoroughly the doctrine of the fall, or else they think that when Adam fell down he broke his little finger, and did not break his neck and ruin his race."

C.H. Spurgeon

"As glowing oven is Thy wrath,
As flame by furious blast upblown;
With equal heat Thy love breaks forth,
Like wall of fire around Thine own."

"I could tell of men who carry knowledge like a sword, They listen to the sermon, and when they meet some friend who gained a little good from it, they will cavil. They say, 'Oh, the first or the third point I did not think quite sound.' *They will be sure to have something to say that will knock the bread from the mouths of those who are willing to feed.*"

"The man who never reads will never be read; he who never quotes will never be quoted. He who will not use the thoughts of other men's brains, proves that he has no brains of his own."

C.H.S.

"It is to be feared that the church of the present day, through a craving for excessive propriety, is growing too artificial; so that enquirers' cries and believers' shouts would be silenced if they were heard in our assemblies. This may be better than boisterous fanaticism, but there is as much danger in the one direction as the other. For our part, we are touched to the heart by a little sacred excess, and when godly men in their joy overleap the narrow bounds of decorum, we do not, like Michal, Saul's daughter, eye them with a sneering heart."

"The Lord hath made known His salvation." — Psalm 98:2

"The Lord is to be praised not only for effecting human salvation, but also for making it known, for man would never have discovered it for himself; nay, not so much as one single soul would ever have found out for himself the way of mercy through a Mediator; in every case it is a Divine Revelation to the mind and heart. In God's own light is His light seen."

"I, for one, feel something like Robin Hood, who never received a man into his company till he had played him at quarter-staff. Honest controversy affords us healthy exercise; besides, it tries the joints of our harness, and lets us know where our weak points may be."

C.H. Spurgeon